Keepsake Baby Quilts
From Scraps™

Designs by Julie Higgins

HOUSE of
WHITE
BIRCHES
PUBLISHERS
SINCE 1947

Introduction

Much like the quilts I designed and stitched for my first book, in 2006, *Keepsake Quilts for Baby*, *Keepsake Baby Quilts From Scraps* was created with the same quest for softness and "Sunday-best" appeal. The difference is, this book includes even more quilts, as well as some very appealing and fun matching accessories. Many of the patterns can be stitched by beginners.

Throughout history, quilters have lovingly created heirloom quilts from the scraps they had on hand. With the current economic times, these scrappy designs will give you an opportunity to use those bits and pieces of fabric that you already have.

Scraps or precuts can be used in nearly every quilt. If you are new to quilting and are short on scraps, some designs use popular Jelly Roll™ strips or charm squares to create the scrappy look. You may mention your lack of scraps to a seasoned quilter, and you might get more than you wished for!

Whatever fabrics you use to create these designs, you can be assured the recipient of your loving labor will cherish these keepsakes for Baby many years down the road.

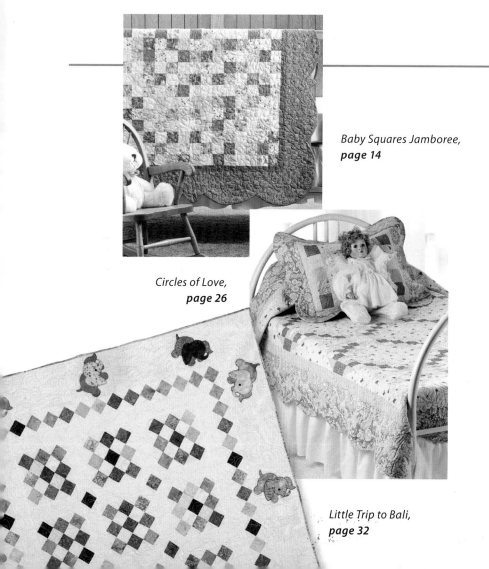

Baby Squares Jamboree,
page 14

Circles of Love,
page 26

Little Trip to Bali,
page 32

Table of Contents

Meet the Designer

Julie Higgins started sewing garments when she was 12 years old. She began making quilts around 2000, found out she loved them and won her first award in 2003. She loves designing and sewing everything from traditional quilts to art quilts and even portraits in fabric. She enjoys presenting to groups of quilters and teaching when her schedule allows.

Julie's first book, *Learn English Paper Piecing by Machine*, was released by House of White Birches in June 2005. Two more books, *Creative Fabric Weaving* and *Keepsake Quilts for Baby* were released by the same publisher in 2006.

Her designs have been published in *McCall's Quick Quilts*, *McCall's Quilting*, *Quilting Arts Magazine*, *Soft Dolls and Animals*, *Quilt Works Today* and *Miniature Quilts*.

Julie lives with her husband, daughter and too many furry friends on the beautiful shores of Lake Lemon, located near Unionville, Ind. She can be contacted by e-mail at higgins9055@comcast.net. She would love to see what you do with her designs!

Dedication

Thanks go out to everyone—family and friends—who continue to encourage me in my craft. My husband Roger, and our daughter, Becky, continue to overlook my "treasures" stacked throughout the house, and for this I am grateful. They even helped me squeeze a 14-foot Gammill into the house (no easy feat), and it's proven to be more fun than I can describe! Let's just say it's like trading in your VW for a Corvette.

Thank you so much to my editor, Jeanne Stauffer, and all of the good staff at House of White Birches. I always enjoy working with you! And you still make me look good.

My friends in the Bloomington Quilter's Guild are awesome! Serving as president this past year was wonderful. Our guild has 200 of the most talented and generous quilters—always willing to volunteer their time and share their knowledge with the community and with each other. Our Web site can be viewed at www.bloomingtonquilters.com. I hope you will visit.

House of White Birches, Berne, Indiana 46711   Clotilde.com

A Star is Born!

Reproductions of fabrics from the 1930s are very popular for use in baby quilts because of their bright, cheery prints and colors.

Project Notes

Select scraps in coordinating colors, in this case pastel, and combine with white solid and a small yellow check to tie it all together.

Appliqué more star shapes to the wide border strips to add lots more color to this whimsical baby quilt.

Project Specifications

- Skill Level: Beginner
- Quilt Size: 42" x 42"
- Block Size: 5" x 5"
- Number of Blocks: 25

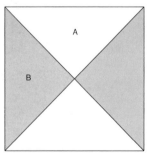

Triangles
5" x 5" Block
Make 13

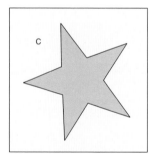

Star
5" x 5" Block
Make 12

Materials

- 7 (6¼" x 6¼") B squares pastel scraps
- 12 (5" x 5") squares pastel scraps
- 36 (2⅞" x 2⅞") J squares pastel scraps
- 1⅛ yards yellow check
- 1¼ yards white solid
- Batting 48" x 48"
- Backing 48" x 48"
- All-purpose thread to match fabrics
- Lavender variegated thread
- Quilting thread
- ½ yard 18"-wide fusible web
- ½ yard fabric stabilizer
- Basting spray
- Basic sewing tools and supplies

Cutting

1. Trace star shape given onto the paper side of the fusible web as directed; cut out shapes, leaving a margin around each one.

2. Fuse the shapes to the wrong side of the 5" x 5" pastel scraps. Cut out shapes on traced lines; remove paper backing.

3. Cut two 5½" by fabric width strips yellow check; subcut strips into (12) 5½" C squares.

4. Cut two 3" x 25½" D strips and two 3" x 30½" E strips yellow check. Cut eight 2½" x 2½" H squares from remainder of these strips.

5. Cut five 2¼" by fabric width strips yellow check for binding.

6. Cut two 6¼" by fabric width strips white solid; subcut strips into seven 6¼" A squares.

7. Cut two 4½" x 30½" F strips and two 4½" x 38½" G strips white solid.

8. Cut three 2⅞" by fabric width strips white solid; subcut strips into (36) 2⅞" I squares.

Completing the Triangles Blocks

1. Draw a diagonal line from corner to corner on the wrong side of the A squares.

2. Place an A square right sides together with a B square; sew ¼" on each side of the marked line as shown in Figure 1.

Figure 1

3. Cut the square in half on the marked line; press open with seam toward B.

4. Repeat steps 2–3 to complete 14 units.

5. Draw a diagonal line on half the stitched units as shown in Figure 2; pair the marked units with different-color unmarked units with the white half right sides together with a colored half as shown in Figure 3.

Figure 2

Figure 3

Completing the Top

1. Join three Triangles blocks with two Star blocks to make an X row as shown in Figure 5; press seams toward Triangles blocks. Repeat to make three X rows.

Figure 5

6. Sew ¼" on each side of the marked line, again referring to Figure 3; cut apart on the marked line to create two Triangles blocks as shown in Figure 4. Press seams in one direction. Repeat to make 13 blocks.

Figure 4

Complete the Star Blocks

1. Center and fuse a star shape on each C square.

2. Cut fabric stabilizer into (12) 5" x 5" squares. Spray-baste a square of stabilizer to the wrong side of each C square.

3. Machine zigzag-stitch around each appliqué shape using lavender variegated thread in the top of the machine and all-purpose thread to match C in the bobbin; remove fabric stabilizer to complete 12 Star blocks.

2. Join three Star blocks with two Triangles blocks to make a Y row, again referring to Figure 5; press seams toward Triangles blocks. Repeat to make two Y rows.

3. Join the rows referring to the Placement Diagram for positioning; press seams in one direction.

4. Sew a D strip to the top and bottom and E strips to opposite sides of the pieced center; press seams toward D and E strips.

5. Sew F strips to the top and bottom and G strips to the opposite sides of the pieced center; press seams toward F and G strips.

6. Draw a diagonal line from corner to corner on the wrong side of each I square.

7. Place an I square right sides together with a J square; stitch ¼" on each side of the marked line as shown in Figure 6. Cut apart on the marked line, open units and press seams toward J to complete two I-J units, again referring to Figure 6. Repeat to make 72 I-J units.

Figure 6

8. Join nine I-J units to make an I-J strip as shown in Figure 7; press seams in one direction. Repeat to make four I-J strips and four reversed I-J strips, again referring to Figure 7.

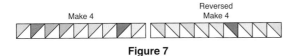

Figure 7

9. Join I-J and reversed I-J strips with an H square to make a side strip as shown in Figure 8; press seams toward H. Repeat to make four side strips.

Figure 8

10. Sew a side strip to opposite sides of the pieced center, referring to the Placement Diagram for positioning; press seams toward G strips.

11. Sew an H square to each end of each remaining side strip; press seams away from H squares.

12. Sew the side/H strips to the top and bottom of the pieced center; press seams toward F strips to complete the pieced top.

Completing the Quilt

1. Sandwich the batting between the completed top and prepared backing; pin or baste layers together to hold.

2. Quilt as desired by hand or machine; remove pins or basting. Trim excess backing and batting even with quilt top.

3. Join binding strips on short ends with diagonal seams to make one long strip; trim seams to ¼" and press seams open. Fold the strip in half along length with wrong sides together; press.

4. Sew binding to the right side of the quilt edges, overlapping ends.

5. Fold binding to the back side and hand-stitch in place to finish. ❖

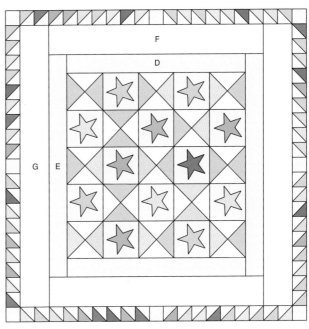

A Star is Born!
Placement Diagram 42" x 42"

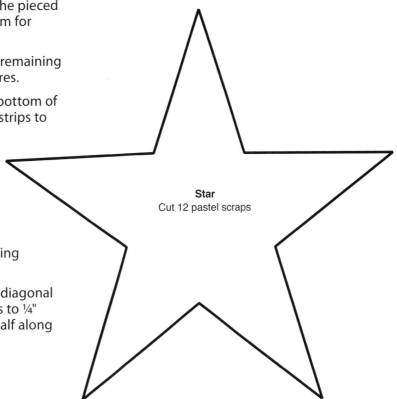

Star
Cut 12 pastel scraps

House of White Birches, Berne, Indiana 46711 Clotilde.com

Baby Charmers

Make a quilt just right for a newborn girl or boy by changing the main colors.

Project Notes

If you have lots of small scrap squares, this pattern is a great place to use them. Be sure to select squares that provide contrast in each block.

The quilts shown were made using two 5" charm packs. Divide the packs into one 16-charm squares stack of girl colors and one 16-charm squares stack of boy colors. The leftover stack can always be used to make another quilt.

Flannel backings were used on both quilts to provide warmth and a soft touch.

Whether you choose to finish your quilt edge with a ruffle or prairie points, this simple quilt design is sure to please.

Baby Charmers Pink

Project Specifications
Skill Level: Beginner
Quilt Size: 28" x 36¼"
Block Size: 4" x 4"
Number of Blocks: 15

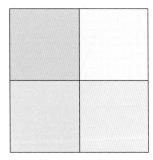

Four-Patch Pink
4" x 4" Block
Make 15

Materials
- 8 each 5" x 5" pink and green charm squares
- ⅜ yard optional binding fabric
- ½ yard pink stripe
- ¾ yard light yellow print
- ⅞ yard pink print for ruffle
- Batting 35" x 43"
- Flannel backing 35" x 43"

- All-purpose thread to match fabrics
- Quilting thread
- Basic sewing tools and supplies

Cutting

1. Cut one 7" by fabric width strip light yellow print; subcut strip into six 7" squares. Cut each square on both diagonals to make 24 C triangles.

2. Cut one 3¾" by fabric width strip light yellow print; subcut strip into four 3¾" squares. Cut each square in half on one diagonal to make 12 D triangles.

3. Cut two 3" x 31¾" G strips light yellow print.

4. Cut two 3" x 28½" H strips light yellow print.

5. Cut four 2" x 28¾" E strips pink stripe.

6. Cut two 2" x 23⅜" F strips pink stripe.

7. Cut six 4½" by fabric width strips pink print for ruffle.

8. Cut four 2¼" by fabric width strips binding fabric for optional binding.

Completing the Blocks

1. Divide the charm squares into one pink A stack and one green B stack; cut each square in half to make two 2½" x 5" strips each square.

2. Select one strip from each stack; sew strips together on the 5" edge. Press seam toward the darker fabric.

3. Cut each stitched strip in half to make two two-patch units as shown in Figure 1.

Figure 1   **Figure 2**

4. Join two different units to complete one Four-Patch Pink block as shown in Figure 2; press seam in one direction.

5. Repeat steps 2–4 to complete 15 Four-Patch Pink blocks.

Completing the Top

1. Sew C to opposite sides of a Four-Patch Pink block as shown in Figure 3; press seams away from C. Repeat to make nine C/block units.

Figure 3

2. Sew D to two adjacent sides and C to one side of each remaining Four-Patch Pink block to make a C-D/block unit as shown in Figure 4. Repeat to make six C-D/block units.

Figure 4

3. Join three C/block units with two C-D/block units to make a block row as shown in Figure 5; press seams in one direction. Repeat to make three block rows.

Figure 5

4. Join the block rows with the four E strips; press seams toward E strips.

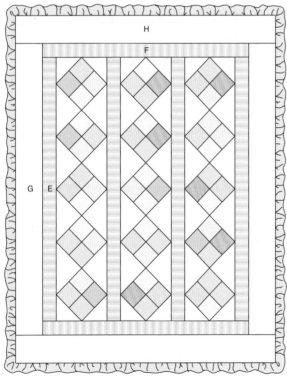

Baby Charmers Pink
Placement Diagram 28" x 36¼"
without ruffle

5. Sew an F strip to the top and bottom of the pieced section; press seams toward F strips.

6. Sew G strips to opposite sides and H strips to the top and bottom of the pieced section to complete the pieced top; press seams toward G and H strips.

Completing the Quilt

1. Sandwich the batting between the completed top and prepared backing; pin or baste layers together to hold.

2. Quilt as desired by hand or machine, leaving the borders unquilted for ruffle finish. *Note: If binding edges, remove pins or basting. Trim excess backing and batting even with quilt top. Prepare binding and bind edges to finish.*

Ruffle Edge Finish

1. Pull the quilt backing out of the way and baste the outside edge of the quilt top to the batting. For the next steps, pin or baste the quilt backing away from the border area—do not catch the backing in the stitching.

2. Trim selvage ends off the ruffle strips; join strips on short ends to make a very large circle; press seams open.

3. Press the circular strip in half with wrong sides together to make a double-layered circle.

4. Use two pins to mark the halfway points in the circle as shown in Figure 6.

Figure 6

5. Using a machine basting stitch, sew two lines of basting stitches close together close to the raw edges of the folded circular strip. *Note: Try to keep the lines of stitching within the ¼" seam allowance as shown in Figure 7.*

Seam allowance

Figure 7

6. Pin the ruffle raw edge to the raw edge of the right side of the quilt top. Match the pins to two diagonal corners of the quilt and at the corners.

7. Pulling the bobbin thread of the basting stitches, gather the ruffle between the pins, distributing full-ness evenly but leaving extra fullness at corners for rounding. Pin the ruffle to the top of the quilt every 1" to 2", matching raw edges of ruffle and quilt border. Repeat for the remaining half of the ruffle.

8. Stitch ruffle to quilt, sewing only through the ruffle, quilt top and batting—do not catch the backing in the stitching. Trim batting even with edge of ruffle/quilt top edge.

9. Remove pins or basting from backing. Smooth out backing and trim backing fabric ½" beyond quilt edge; press ruffle away from the quilt top and seam allowance to the quilt back.

10. On the back of the quilt, press under ½" of backing, making a finished edge that is even with the front side of the quilt. Pin in place; hand- or machine-stitch in place from the top side of the quilt close to the edge as shown in Figure 8.

Figure 8

11. Quilt the outside border as desired by hand or machine to finish.

Baby Charmers Blue

Project Specifications
Skill Level: Beginner
Quilt Size: 28" x 36¼"
Block Size: 4" x 4"
Number of Blocks: 15

Four-Patch Blue
4" x 4" Block
Make 15

Materials
- 8 each 5" x 5" blue and yellow charm squares
- ⅜ yard optional binding fabric
- ½ yard blue stripe
- ¾ yard light yellow print
- ⅞ yard or 36 (5") blue charm squares for prairie points

- Batting 35" x 43"
- Flannel backing 35" x 43"
- All-purpose thread to match fabrics
- Quilting thread
- Basic sewing tools and supplies

Cutting
1. Cut one 7" by fabric width strip light yellow print; subcut strip into six 7" squares. Cut each square on both diagonals to make 24 C triangles.

2. Cut one 3¾" by fabric width strip light yellow print; subcut strip into four 3¾" squares. Cut each square in half on one diagonal to make 12 D triangles.

3. Cut two 3" x 31¾" G strips light yellow print.

4. Cut two 3" x 28½" H strips light yellow print.

5. Cut four 2" x 28¾" E strips blue or pink stripe.

6. Cut two 2" x 23½" F strips blue stripe.

7. Cut four 2¼" by fabric width strips binding fabric for optional binding.

Completing the Blocks
1. Divide the charm squares into one blue A stack and one yellow B stack; cut each square in half to make two 2½" x 5" strips each square.

2. Select one strip from each stack; sew strips together on the 5" edge. Press seam toward the darker fabric.

3. Cut each stitched strip in half to make two two-patch units as shown in Figure 9.

| Figure 9 | Figure 10 |

4. Join two different units to complete one Four-Patch Blue block as shown in Figure 10; press seam in one direction.

5. Repeat steps 2–4 to complete 15 Four-Patch Blue blocks.

Completing the Top
1. Sew C to opposite sides of a Four-Patch Blue block as shown in Figure 11; press seams away from C. Repeat to make nine C/block units.

Figure 11

2. Sew D to two adjacent sides and C to one side of each remaining Four-Patch Blue block to make a C-D/block unit as shown in Figure 12. Repeat to make six C-D/block units.

Figure 12

3. Join three C/block units with two C-D/block units to make a block row as shown in Figure 13; press seams in one direction. Repeat to make three block rows.

Figure 13

4. Join the block rows with the four E strips; press seams toward E strips.

5. Sew an F strip to the top and bottom of the pieced section; press seams toward F strips.

6. Sew G strips to opposite long sides and H strips to the top and bottom of the pieced section to complete the pieced top; press seams toward G and H strips.

Completing the Quilt

1. Sandwich the batting between the completed top and prepared backing; pin or baste layers together to hold.

2. Quilt as desired by hand or machine, leaving the borders unquilted for prairie-point finish. *Note: If binding edges, remove pins or basting. Trim excess backing and batting even with quilt top. Prepare binding and bind edges to finish.*

Prairie Point Edge Finish

1. Press each of the (36) 5" charm squares in half on one diagonal; fold in half again and press as shown in Figure 14. *Note: You now have a triangle with four layers of fabric. Looking at the triangles with the long edge on the bottom you have one folded side and one open side.*

Figure 14

2. Evenly space eight folded triangles, matching raw edges on the top and bottom edges of the quilt top, placing the folded edge of one prairie point into the adjacent prairie point's opening as shown

in Figure 15. Repeat with 10 folded triangles on each long side of the quilt top. Machine-baste to hold in place.

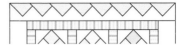

Figure 15

3. Trim backing fabric ½" beyond quilt edge; press prairie points up to the outside of the quilt and seam allowance to the back of the quilt.

4. On the back of the quilt, press under ½" of backing, making a finished edge that is even with the front side of the quilt. Pin in place; hand- or machine-stitch in place from the top side of the quilt close to the edge as shown in Figure 16.

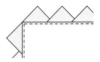

Figure 16

5. Quilt the outside border as desired by hand or machine to finish. ❖

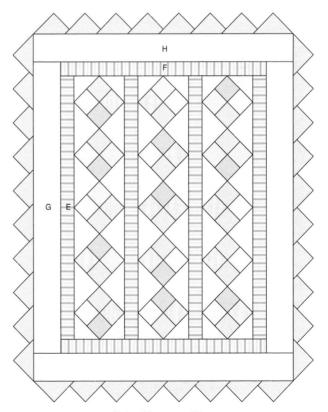

Baby Charmers Blue
Placement Diagram 28" x 36¼"
without prairie points

Baby Squares Jamboree

Use up leftover Jelly Roll™ strips to make a delicious little quilt for Baby.

Project Specifications
Skill Level: Beginner
Quilt Size: 44" x 54"

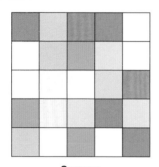

Squares
10" x 10" Block
Make 12

Materials
- 20 (2½" by fabric width) Jelly Roll strips or strips from your stash
- ¼ yard rust tonal
- 1⅜ yards coral print
- Batting 50" x 60"
- Backing 50" x 60"
- All-purpose thread to match fabrics
- Quilting thread
- Basic sewing tools and supplies

Cutting
1. Cut two 1½" x 40½" B strips and two 1½" x 32½" C strips rust tonal.

2. Cut two 6½" x 42½" D and two 6½" x 44½" E strips along the length of the coral print.

3. Cut and piece 2¼"-wide bias strips coral print to total 225".

Completing the Squares Blocks
1. Cut the 2½" by fabric-width strips in half to make two 21"-long strips from each strip.

2. Select five 21"-long strips; sew together along length to make a strip set; press seams in one direction. Repeat to make eight strip sets.

3. Subcut strip sets into a total of (60) 2½" A units as shown in Figure 1.

Figure 1

4. Select five different A units; join together along length to complete one Squares block with seams of adjacent rows pressed in opposite directions. Press seams in one direction.

5. Repeat step 4 to complete 12 Squares blocks.

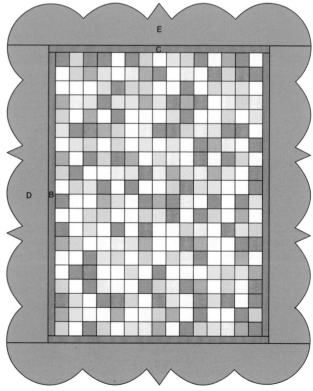

Baby Squares Jamboree
Placement Diagram 44" x 54"

Completing the Top

1. Join three blocks to make a row; press seams in one direction. Repeat to make four rows.

2. Join the rows with seams in adjacent rows pressed in opposite directions; press seams in one direction.

3. Sew B strips to opposite sides and C strips to the top and bottom of the pieced top; press seams toward B and C strips.

4. Sew D strips to opposite long sides and E strips to the top and bottom of the pieced center to complete the pieced top; press seams toward D and E strips.

Completing the Quilt

1. Sandwich the batting between the completed top and prepared backing; pin or baste layers together to hold.

2. Quilt as desired by hand or machine; remove pins or basting. Trim excess backing and batting even with quilt top.

3. Make a template for the scallop and points using patterns given; center and mark a scallop pattern in the center of each side border. Mark a side point on each side of the marked scallop, and mark another scallop on each end as shown in Figure 2.

Figure 2

4. Mark an end point in the center of the top and bottom borders; mark a scallop on each side of the point as shown in Figure 3.

Figure 3

5. Use a large plate or pizza pan to mark corner curves, connecting to the last scallop on each edge as shown in Figure 4.

Figure 4

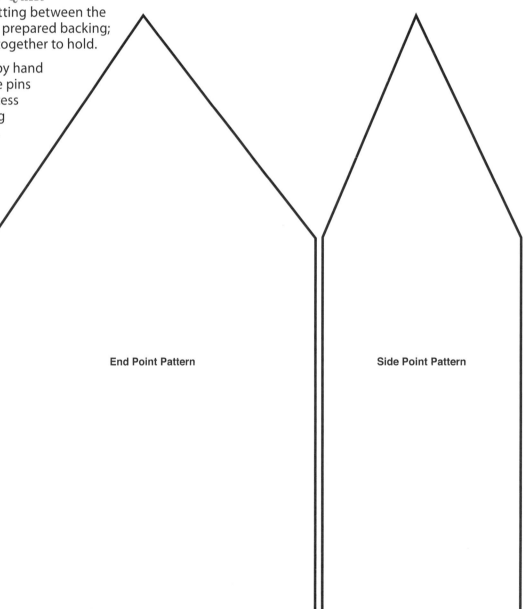

End Point Pattern

Side Point Pattern

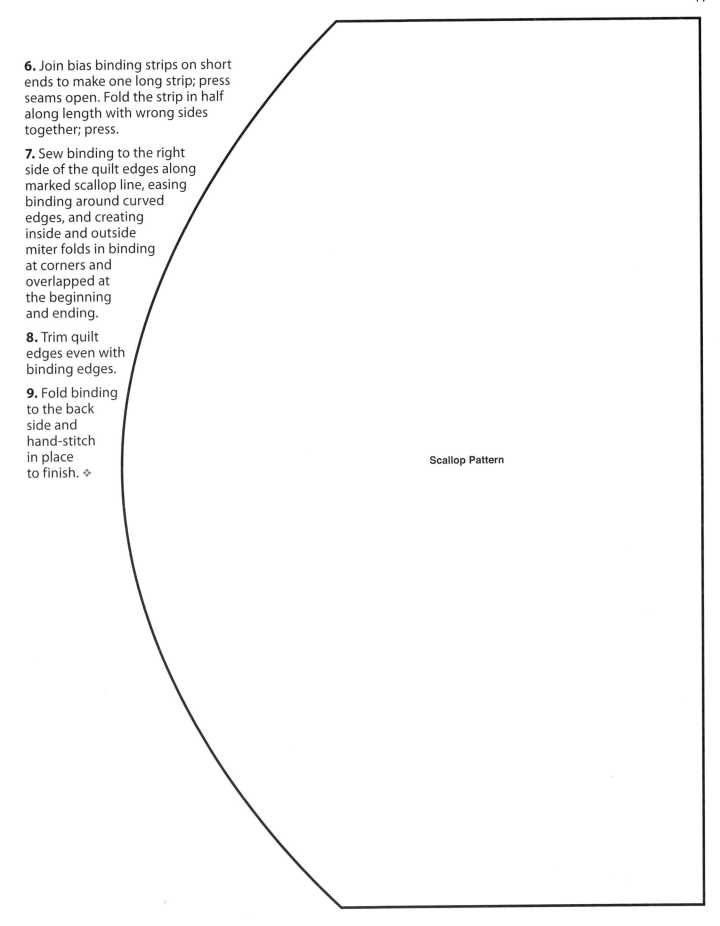

6. Join bias binding strips on short ends to make one long strip; press seams open. Fold the strip in half along length with wrong sides together; press.

7. Sew binding to the right side of the quilt edges along marked scallop line, easing binding around curved edges, and creating inside and outside miter folds in binding at corners and overlapped at the beginning and ending.

8. Trim quilt edges even with binding edges.

9. Fold binding to the back side and hand-stitch in place to finish. ❖

Scallop Pattern

House of White Birches, Berne, Indiana 46711 Clotilde.com

Joyful Amish Sparkle

Solid colors with black give this baby quilt an Amish look.
Make a miniature version as a matching doll quilt.

Project Specifications
Skill Level: Beginner
Quilt Size: 41½" x 50"
Block Size: 6" x 6"
Number of Blocks: 12

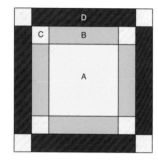

Amish Squares
6" x 6" Block
Make 12

Materials
• Scraps medium and dark solids
• ⅜ yard black solid
• ⅔ yard gray solid
• 1⅞ yards blue solid
• Batting 48" x 56"
• Backing 48" x 56"
• All-purpose thread to match fabrics
• Quilting thread
• Basic sewing tools and supplies

Cutting
1. Cut (12) 3½" x 3½" A squares solid scraps.

2. Cut 12 sets of four same-fabric 1¼" x 3½" B rectangles solid scraps.

3. Cut three 1¼" by fabric width strips gray solid; subcut strips into (96) 1¼" C squares.

4. Cut two 5⅛" x 5⅛" squares gray solid; cut each square in half on one diagonal to make four G triangles.

5. Cut two 2½" x 34½" H strips and two 2½" x 30" I strips gray solid.

6. Cut one 6½" by fabric width strip blue solid; subcut strips into six 6½" E squares.

7. Cut one 9¾" by fabric width strip blue solid; subcut strips into three 9¾" squares. Cut each square on both diagonals to make 12 F triangles; discard two triangles.

8. Cut two 6½" x 38½" K strips and two 6½" x 42" L strips blue solid.

9. Cut one 6½" by fabric width strip blue solid; subcut strip into four 6½" J squares.

10. Cut five 2¼" by fabric width strips blue solid for binding.

11. Cut eight 1¼" by fabric width strips black solid; subcut strips into (48) 5" D strips.

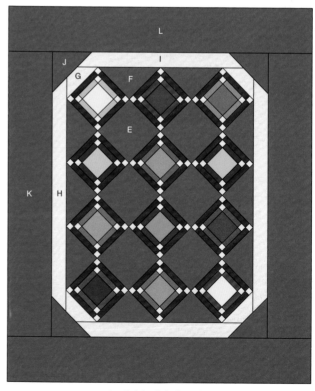

Joyful Amish Sparkle
Placement Diagram 41½" x 50"

Completing the Amish Squares Blocks

1. To complete one Amish Squares block, select one set of four same-fabric B strips. Sew B to opposite sides of A; press seams toward B.

2. Sew C to each end of the two remaining B strips; press seams toward B.

3. Sew a B-C strip to the remaining sides of A; press seams toward the B-C strips.

4. Sew D to opposite sides of the pieced unit; press seams toward D.

5. Sew C to each end of each remaining D strip; press seams toward D.

6. Sew a C-D strip to the remaining sides of the pieced unit to complete one Amish Squares block; press seams toward the C-D strips.

7. Repeat steps 1–6 to complete 12 Amish Squares blocks.

House of White Birches, Berne, Indiana 46711 Clotilde.com

Completing the Top

1. Join two E squares, three Amish Square blocks and one each F and G triangles to make a G row as shown in Figure 1; press seams away from blocks. Repeat to make two G rows.

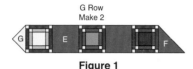

Figure 1

2. Join two Amish Square blocks with one E square and two F triangles to make an F row as shown in Figure 2; press seams away from blocks. Repeat to make two F rows.

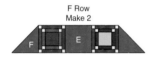

Figure 2   **Figure 3**

3. Sew an F triangle to opposite sides of one block; add G to one remaining side as shown in Figure 3 to complete a corner unit. Press seams away from the block. Repeat to make two corner units.

4. Join the rows and corner units referring to Figure 4; press seams in one direction.

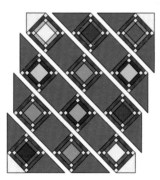

Figure 4

5. Sew H strips to opposite long sides and I strips to the top and bottom of the pieced center; press seams toward H and I strips.

6. Mark a diagonal line from corner to corner on the wrong side of each J square.

7. Place a J square right sides together on one corner of the pieced center; stitch on the marked line as shown in Figure 5. Trim seam to ¼" and press J to the right side.

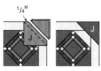

Figure 5

8. Repeat step 7 on each corner of the pieced center.

9. Sew K strips to opposite long sides and L strips to the top and bottom of the pieced center; press seams toward K and L strips to complete the pieced top.

Completing the Quilt

1. Sandwich the batting between the completed top and prepared backing; pin or baste layers together to hold.

2. Quilt as desired by hand or machine; remove pins or basting. Trim excess backing and batting even with quilt top.

3. Join binding strips on short ends with diagonal seams to make one long strip; trim seams to ¼" and press seams open. Fold the strip in half along length with wrong sides together; press.

4. Stitch binding to the right side of the quilt edges, overlapping ends.

5. Fold binding to the back side and hand-stitch in place to finish.

Miniature Joyful Amish Sparkle

Project Specifications
Skill Level: Beginner
Quilt Size: 20¾" x 25"
Block Size: 3" x 3"
Number of Blocks: 12

Amish Squares
3" x 3" Block
Make 12

Materials
- Scraps medium and dark solids
- ¼ yard black solid
- ⅓ yard gray solid
- 1 yard blue solid
- Batting 27" x 31"
- Backing 27" x 31"
- All-purpose thread to match fabrics
- Quilting thread
- Basic sewing tools and supplies

Cutting
1. Cut (12) 2" x 2" A squares solid scraps.

2. Cut 12 sets of four same-fabric ⅞" x 2" B rectangles solid scraps.

3. Cut two ⅞" by fabric width strips gray solid; subcut strips into (96) ⅞" C squares.

4. Cut two 3" x 3" squares gray solid; cut each square in half on one diagonal to make four G triangles.

5. Cut two 1½" x 17½" H strips and two 1½" x 16" I strips gray solid.

6. Cut one 3½" by fabric width strip blue solid; subcut strips into six 3½" E and four 3½" J squares.

7. Cut one 5½" by fabric width strip blue solid; subcut strip into three 5½" squares. Cut each square on both diagonals to make 12 F triangles; discard two triangles.

8. Cut two 3½" x 19½" K strips and two 3½" x 21¼" L strips blue solid.

9. Cut three 2¼" by fabric width strips blue solid for binding.

10. Cut four ⅞" by fabric width strips black solid; subcut strips into (48) 2¾" D strips.

Completing the Amish Squares Blocks

1. To complete one Amish Squares block, select one set of four same-fabric B strips. Sew B to opposite sides of A; press seams toward B.

2. Sew C to each end of the two remaining B strips; press seams toward B.

3. Sew a B-C strip to the remaining sides of A; press seams toward the B-C strips.

4. Sew D to opposite sides of the pieced unit; press seams toward D.

5. Sew C to each end of each remaining D strip; press seams toward D.

6. Sew a C-D strip to the remaining sides of the pieced unit to complete one Amish Squares block; press seams toward the C-D strips.

7. Repeat steps 1–6 to complete 12 Amish Squares blocks.

Completing the Top

1. Join two E squares, three Amish Square blocks and one each F and G triangles to make a G row as shown in Figure 1; press seams away from blocks. Repeat to make two G rows.

2. Join two Amish Square blocks with one E square and two F triangles to make an F row as shown in Figure 2; press seams away from blocks. Repeat to make two F rows.

3. Sew an F triangle to opposite sides of one block; add G to one remaining side as shown in Figure 3 to complete a corner unit. Press seams away from the block. Repeat to make two corner units.

4. Join the rows and corner units referring to Figure 4; press seams in one direction.

5. Sew H strips to opposite long sides and I strips to the top and bottom of the pieced center; press seams toward H and I strips.

6. Mark a diagonal line from corner to corner on the wrong side of each J square.

7. Place a J square right sides together on one corner of the pieced center; stitch on the marked line as shown in Figure 5. Trim seam to ¼" and press J to the right side.

8. Repeat step 7 on each corner of the pieced center.

9. Sew K strips to opposite long sides and L strips to the top and bottom of the pieced center; press seams toward K and L strips to complete the pieced top.

Completing the Quilt

1. Sandwich the batting between the completed top and prepared backing; pin or baste layers together to hold.

2. Quilt as desired by hand or machine; remove pins or basting. Trim excess backing and batting even with quilt top.

3. Join binding strips on short ends with diagonal seams to make one long strip; trim seams to ¼" and press seams open. Fold the strip in half along length with wrong sides together; press.

4. Stitch binding to right side of quilt edges, overlapping ends.

5. Fold binding to the back side and hand-stitch in place to finish. ❖

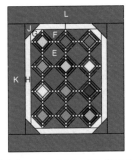

Miniature Joyful Amish Sparkle
Placement Diagram 20¾" x 25"

House of White Birches, Berne, Indiana 46711   Clotilde.com

Baby's Fancy

Using a variation of the traditional Gentleman's Fancy block, this is a great quilt for a beginner.

Project Notes

You may use scraps or coordinated fabrics to make this baby quilt. You may also highlight a focus fabric in the center of each block. Fussy cutting to frame a special motif is also a possibility for the block centers. To make the quilt easier for a beginner, the G star points may be omitted. The E sashing strips may be used as cut if you choose this option.

Project Specifications

Skill Level: Beginner
Quilt Size: 45" x 55½"
Block Size: 9" x 9"
Number of Blocks: 12

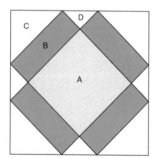

Baby's Fancy
9" x 9" Block
Make 12

Materials

- ½ yard green print
- ⅝ yard brown print
- ⅝ yard brown/white stripe
- ⅞ yard dark brown tonal
- 1½ yards cream tonal
- Batting 51" x 62"
- Backing 51" x 62"
- All-purpose thread to match fabrics
- Quilting thread
- Basic sewing tools and supplies

Cutting

1. Cut two 5¼" by fabric width strips green print; subcut strips into (12) 5¼" A squares.

2. Cut three 5¼" by fabric width strips brown print; subcut strips into (48) 2⅛" B rectangles.

3. Cut three 4¼" by fabric width strips cream tonal; subcut strips into (24) 4¼" squares. Cut each square in half on one diagonal to make 48 C triangles.

4. Cut one 3½" by fabric width strip cream tonal; subcut strip into (12) 3½" squares. Cut each square on both diagonals to make 48 D triangles.

5. Cut six 5" by fabric width L/M strips cream tonal.

6. Cut five 2" by fabric width strips brown/white stripe; subcut strips into (17) 9½" E strips.

7. Cut two 2" x 41" H strips and two 2" x 33½" I strips brown/white stripe.

8. Cut one 2" by fabric width strip dark brown tonal; subcut strip into six 2" x 2" F squares and (15) 1¼" x 1¼" G squares.

9. Cut one 1¼" by fabric width strip dark brown tonal; subcut strip into (33) 1¼" G squares to total 48.

10. Cut two 2" x 36½" K strips and three 2" by fabric width J strips dark brown tonal.

11. Cut six 2¼" by fabric width strips dark brown tonal for binding.

Completing the Blocks

1. To complete one Baby's Fancy block, sew B to opposite sides of A and add C to each B end to complete the center row as shown in Figure 1; press seams toward B. ***Note:*** *When sewing the C pieces to the A-B unit, be sure the triangle points are jutting past the rectangle. To help with this, fold the A-B unit and crease to mark the center; repeat with the C triangle. Match the centers so that an even amount will extend at each end.*

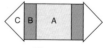

Figure 1

2. Sew C to one long side of two B pieces; press seam toward C.

3. Add D to each end of a B-C unit to complete a corner unit as shown in Figure 2; press seams toward D. Repeat to make two corner units.

Figure 2

4. Sew a corner unit to opposite sides of the center row to complete one Baby's Fancy block referring to the block drawing; press seams toward corner units.

5. Repeat steps 1–4 to complete 12 Baby's Fancy blocks.

Completing the Top

1. Mark a diagonal line from corner to corner on the wrong side of each G square.

2. Place a G square right sides together on one end of an E strip and stitch on the marked line as shown in Figure 3; trim seam to ¼" and press G to the right side, again referring to Figure 3.

Figure 3

3. Repeat steps 2 and 3 with G on the opposite side of the same end of E as shown in Figure 4.

Figure 4

4. Repeat step 2 with G on both ends of seven E strips and on just one end of the remaining 10 E strips referring to Figure 5.

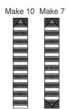

Figure 5

5. Join three blocks with two one-end E-G strips to make an X row as shown in Figure 6; press seams away from the blocks. Repeat to make two X rows.

6. Join three blocks with two both-end E-G strips to make a Y row again referring to Figure 6; press seams away from blocks. Repeat to make two Y rows.

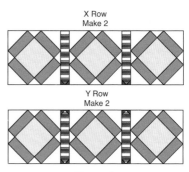

Figure 6

7. Join one two-end E-G strip with two one-end E-G strips and two F squares to make a sashing row as shown in Figure 7; press seams toward F squares. Repeat to make three sashing rows.

Figure 7

8. Join the X and Y rows with the sashing rows referring to the Placement Diagram for positioning of rows; press seams toward sashing rows.

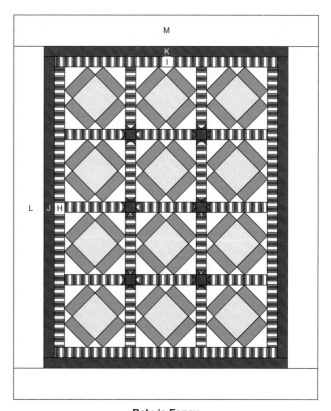

Baby's Fancy
Placement Diagram 45" x 55½"

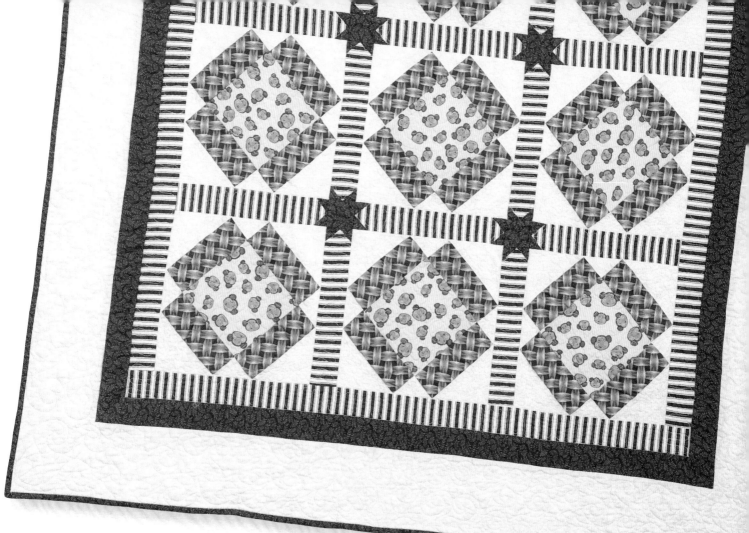

9. Sew an H strip to opposite long sides and I strips to the top and bottom of the pieced center; press seams toward the H and I strips.

10. Join J strips on short ends to make one long strip; press seams open. Subcut strip into two 44" J strips.

11. Sew J strips to opposite long sides and K strips to the top and bottom of the pieced center; press seams toward J and K strips.

Tip

When sewing the G triangles to the E strip, the gray area where the G seams cross should be ¼" as shown in Figure 8.

Figure 8

12. Join the L/M strips on short ends to make one long strip; press seams open. Subcut strip into two 47" L strips and two 45½" M strips.

13. Sew L strips to opposite long sides and M strips to the top and bottom of the pieced center; press seams toward L and M strips to complete the pieced top.

Completing the Quilt

1. Sandwich the batting between the completed top and prepared backing; pin or baste layers together to hold.

2. Quilt as desired by hand or machine; remove pins or basting. Trim excess backing and batting even with quilt top.

3. Join binding strips on short ends with diagonal seams to make one long strip; trim seams to ¼" and press seams open. Fold the strip in half along length with wrong sides together; press.

4. Sew binding to the right side of the quilt edges, overlapping ends. Fold binding to the back side and stitch in place. ❖

Circles of Love

Two blocks combine to create the optical illusion of a curving design. There are no curved seams—it just looks that way!

Circles of Love Quilt

Project Specifications

Skill Level: Intermediate
Quilt Size: 51" x 69"
Block Size: 9" x 9" and 9" x 4½"
Number of Blocks: 15 and 16

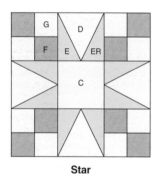

Star
9" x 9" Block
Make 8

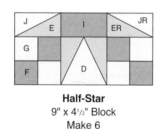

Half-Star
9" x 4½" Block
Make 6

Materials

- ¼ yard yellow tonal
- ⅝ rose tonal
- ¾ yard medium pink print
- ⅞ yard green print
- 1½ yards light pink print
- 2 yards pink floral
- Batting 57" x 75"
- Backing 57" x 75"
- All-purpose thread to match fabrics
- Quilting thread
- Water-soluble marker
- Basic sewing tools and supplies

Cutting

1. Prepare templates for D and E/J using patterns given; cut as directed on each piece.

2. Cut four 9½" by fabric width strips light pink print; subcut strips into seven 9½" A squares, (10) 5" H rectangles and four 5" x 5" K squares.

3. Cut five 2" by fabric width strips each light pink print G strips and rose tonal F strips.

4. Cut one 2" by fabric width strip rose tonal; subcut strip into six 3½" I rectangles.

5. Cut four 3½" by fabric width strips green print; subcut strips into (48) 3½" B squares.

6. Cut three 2" by fabric width L strips green print.

7. Cut two 2" x 39½" M strips green print.

8. Cut six 6½" by fabric width N/O strips pink floral.

9. Cut 2¼"-wide bias strips pink floral to total 260".

10. Cut one 3½" by fabric width strip yellow tonal; subcut strip into eight 3½" C squares.

Completing the Star Blocks

1. Sew an F strip to a G strip with right sides together along length; press seams toward F strip. Repeat to make five F-G strip sets.

2. Subcut the F-G strip sets into (88) 2" F-G units as shown in Figure 1.

Figure 1   **Figure 2**

3. Join two F-G units to make a corner unit as shown in Figure 2; press seam in one direction. Repeat to make 44 corner units; set aside 12 units for Half-Star blocks.

4. Sew E and ER to D to complete a D-E unit as shown in Figure 3; press seams toward E and ER. Repeat to make 32 D-E units.

Figure 3   **Figure 4**

5. To complete one Star block, sew a D-E unit to opposite sides of C to make the center row as shown in Figure 4; press seams toward C.

6. Sew a corner unit to opposite sides of a D-E unit to complete the top row as shown in Figure 5; press seams toward the corner units. Repeat to make the bottom row.

Figure 5

7. Sew the top and bottom rows to the center row referring to the block drawing to complete one Star block; press seam toward the center row.

8. Repeat steps 5–7 to complete eight Star blocks.

Completing the Half-Star Blocks

1. Sew E to J and ER to JR as shown in Figure 6; press seams toward E and ER. Repeat to make six each E-J and ER-JR units.

Figure 6

2. Sew E and ER to D to make a D-E unit, again referring to Figure 3; press seams toward E and ER. Repeat to make six D-E units.

3. To complete one Half-Star block, sew a corner unit to opposite sides of a D-E unit, again referring to Figure 5 to make a row; press seams toward the corner units.

4. Sew an E-J and ER-JR unit to I as shown in Figure 7.

Figure 7

5. Join the two rows to complete one Half-Star block referring to the block drawing.

6. Repeat steps 3–5 to complete six Half-Star blocks.

Completing the Snowball Blocks

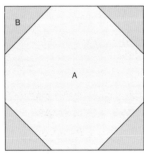

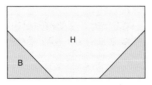

Snowball
9" x 9" Block
Make 7

Half-Snowball
9" x 4¹/₂" Block
Make 10

1. Draw a diagonal line from corner to corner on the wrong side of each B square.

2. Place a B square on one corner of A; stitch on the marked line and trim seam to ¼" as shown in Figure 8.

Figure 8

3. Repeat step 2 on each corner of A to complete a Snowball block referring to the block drawing.

4. Repeat steps 2 and 3 to complete seven Snowball blocks.

Completing the Half-Snowball Blocks

1. Repeat step 2 on two corners of H to complete one Half-Snowball block. Repeat to make 10 Half-Snowball blocks.

Completing the Top

1. Join one K, one Half-Star and two Half-Snowball blocks to make an X row as shown in Figure 9; press seams toward the Half-Snowball blocks. Repeat to make two X rows.

2. Join two Half-Snowball blocks with one Snowball block and two Star blocks to make a Y row, again referring to Figure 9; press seams away from Star blocks. Repeat to make three Y rows.

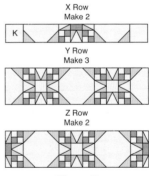

Figure 9

3. Join two Half-Star blocks with two Snowball blocks and one Star block to make a Z row, again referring to Figure 9; press seams toward Snowball blocks. Repeat to make two Z rows.

4. Arrange and join the X, Y and Z rows referring to the Placement Diagram for positioning to complete the pieced center; press seams toward X and Z rows.

5. Join the L strips on short ends to make one long strip; press seam open. Subcut strip into two 54½" L strips.

6. Sew L strips to opposite long sides and M strips to the top and bottom of the pieced center; press seams toward L and M strips.

7. Join the N/O strips on short ends to make one long strip; press seams open. Subcut strip into two 57½" N strips and two 52½" O strips.

8. Sew N strips to opposite long sides and O strips to the top and bottom of the pieced center; press seams toward N and O strips to complete the pieced top.

Completing the Quilt

1. Sandwich the batting between the completed top and prepared backing; pin or baste layers together to hold.

2. Quilt as desired by hand or machine; remove pins or basting. Trim excess backing and batting even with quilt top.

3. Prepare template for scallop using pattern given. Center and mark scallop pattern along the edge of the N/O borders using a water-soluble marker or pencil and referring to the Placement Diagram for positioning. Use a large plate or pizza pan to mark round corners to connect the scallops on each edge.

4. Join bias binding strips on short ends to make one long strip; press seams open. Fold the strip in half along length with wrong sides together; press.

5. Sew binding to the right side of the quilt edges along marked scallop line, overlapping ends.

6. Trim edges even with binding seam edges.

7. Fold binding to the back side and hand-stitch in place to finish.

Pillow Sham

Project Specifications
Skill Level: Intermediate
Sham Size: 23" x 19"

Materials
- 35 assorted 2½" x 2½" A squares to match quilt
- ⅛ yard green print
- ⅓ yard pink floral
- 1 yard muslin
- Batting 29" x 25"
- ⅔ yard backing
- All-purpose thread to match fabrics
- Quilting thread
- 16" x 12" travel-size pillow form
- Basic sewing tools and supplies

Cutting
1. Cut two 1½" by fabric width strips green print; subcut strips into two 10½" B strips and two 16½" C strips.

2. Cut two 4" by fabric width strips pink floral; subcut strips into two 12½" D strips and two 23½" E strips.

3. Cut two 19½" x 16" backing pieces from backing fabric.

4. Cut one 29" x 25" piece muslin.

Circles of Love
Placement Diagram 51" x 69"

House of White Birches, Berne, Indiana 46711   Clotilde.com

Completing the Sham

1. Arrange and join the A squares in five rows of seven squares each; press seams in adjoining rows in opposite directions.

2. Join the rows; press seams in one direction.

3. Sew B strips to opposite short ends and C strips to the long sides of the pieced center; press seams toward B and C strips.

4. Sew D strips to opposite short ends and E strips to the long sides of the pieced center; press seams toward D and E strips.

5. Sandwich batting between the completed top and the muslin rectangle; pin or baste to hold.

6. Quilt as desired by hand or machine; remove pins or basting when quilting is complete.

7. Prepare templates for sham scallops using patterns given.

8. Center and trace a sham end scallop pattern on each short end and two sham side scallops on the long sides of the muslin side of the quilted top. Use a large plate to mark round corners to connect the scallops.

9. Turn under one 19" edge of each backing piece ¼"; press. Fold under ¼" again, press and stitch to hem. Repeat on the second backing piece.

10. Place hemmed backing pieces right sides together with the quilted top, overlapping backing pieces as shown in Figure 10; stitch all around on the marked scallop lines. Clip curves and indents; turn right side out through overlapped opening. Press edges flat.

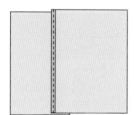
Figure 10

11. Stitch in the ditch between seams of the B/D and C/E borders to create a flange as shown in Figure 11.

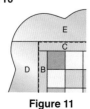
Figure 11

12. Topstitch close to curved edges all around to complete the pillow sham. Insert pillow through back openings to use. ❖

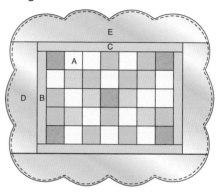

Pillow Sham
Placement Diagram 23" x 19"

Quilt Scallop Pattern

Place line on fold

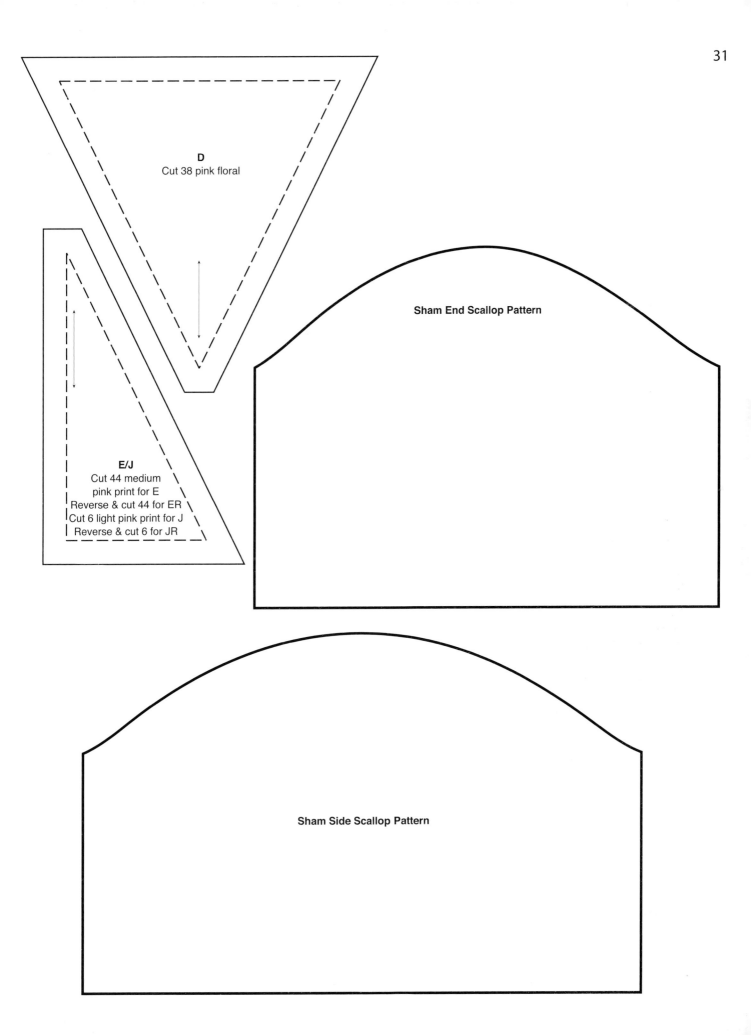

D
Cut 38 pink floral

E/J
Cut 44 medium
pink print for E
Reverse & cut 44 for ER
Cut 6 light pink print for J
Reverse & cut 6 for JR

Sham End Scallop Pattern

Sham Side Scallop Pattern

Little Trip to Bali

Showcase batik scraps in a little bejeweled quilt with the flavors of Bali using Trip Around the World blocks.

Project Specifications
Skill Level: Intermediate
Quilt Size: 46½" x 46½"
Block Size: 6⅞" x 6⅞" and 6" x 6"
Number of Blocks: 9 and 12

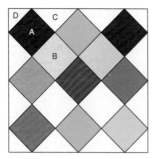

Trip Around the World
6⅞" x 6⅞" Block
Make 9

Elephant
6" x 6" Block
Make 12

Materials
- ¼ yard total pastel batik scraps
- ½ yard multicolored batik print
- 1 yard total dark batik scraps
- 2¼ yards light mottled batik
- Batting 53" x 53"
- Backing 53" x 53"
- All-purpose thread to match fabrics
- Dark-color variegated thread
- Quilting thread
- 1 yard 18"-wide fusible web
- ⅞ yard fabric stabilizer
- Basting spray
- Black fine-tip fabric pen
- Basic sewing tools and supplies

Cutting
1. Cut (137) total 2⅛" x 2⅛" A squares dark batik scraps.

2. Cut (36) 2⅛" x 2⅛" B squares pastel batik scraps.

3. Cut four 3½" by fabric width strips light mottled batik; subcut strips into (44) 3½" squares. Cut each square on both diagonals to make 176 C triangles.

4. Cut two 2" by fabric width strips light mottled batik; subcut strips into (34) 2" squares. Cut each square in half on one diagonal to make 68 D triangles.

5. Cut one 7⅜" by fabric width strip light mottled batik; subcut strip into (12) 2⅞" E strips.

6. Cut two 2¾" x 25⅞" F strips light mottled batik.

7. Cut two 2¾" x 30⅜" G strips light mottled batik.

8. Cut two 7" by fabric width strips light mottled batik; subcut strips into (12) 7" H squares.

9. Cut three 6½" by fabric width strips light mottled batik; subcut strips into eight 8¾" I rectangles and four 6½" J squares.

10. Cut five 2¼" by fabric width strips multicolored batik print for binding.

11. Trace each elephant shape onto the paper side of the fusible web as directed; cut out shapes, leaving a margin around each one.

12. Fuse the shapes to the wrong side of fabrics as directed. Cut out shapes on traced lines; remove paper backing.

Completing the Trip Around the World Blocks
1. To complete one Trip Around the World block, join three A and two B squares to make the center diagonal row; add D to each end as shown in Figure 1; press seams toward A.

Figure 1

2. Repeat step 1 with one B and two A squares, adding C to each end to make a side row as shown in Figure 2; press seams toward A. Repeat to make a second side row.

Figure 2

3. Sew C to two opposite sides and D to one side of A to complete a corner unit as shown in Figure 3; repeat to make two corner units.

Figure 3

4. Sew the side rows to the center diagonal row as shown in Figure 4; press seams away from the center diagonal row.

Figure 4

5. Sew a corner unit to each side row, again referring to Figure 4, to complete one Trip Around the World block; press seams toward corner units.

6. Repeat steps 1–5 to complete nine Trip Around the World Blocks.

Completing the Elephant Blocks

1. Fold each H square in half on the vertical and horizontal and crease to mark the centers.

2. Center and fuse an elephant motif on each H square with pieces fused in numerical order.

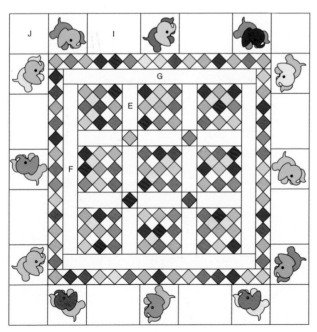

Little Trip to Bali
Placement Diagram 46¹⁄₂" x 46¹⁄₂"

3. Cut fabric stabilizer into (12) 6" x 6" squares. Spray-baste a square of stabilizer to the wrong side of each H square.

4. Machine zigzag-stitch around each appliqué shape using a dark-color variegated thread in the top of the machine and all-purpose thread to match H in the bobbin; remove fabric stabilizer when stitching is complete.

5. Using the black fine-point fabric pen, add an eye circle to each elephant referring to pattern for size and positioning.

6. Trim block to 6¹⁄₂" x 6¹⁄₂", centering elephant motifs, to complete 12 Elephant blocks.

Completing the Top

1. Join three Trip Around the World blocks with two E strips to make a block row; press seams toward E strips. Repeat to make three block rows.

2. Sew D to each side of A to make an A-D unit as shown in Figure 5; press seams toward D. Repeat to make four A-D units.

Figure 5

3. Join three E strips with two A-D units to make a sashing row as shown in Figure 6; press seams toward E strips. Repeat to make two sashing strips.

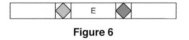

Figure 6

4. Join the block rows with the sashing rows to complete the pieced center; press seams toward the sashing rows.

5. Sew F strips to opposite sides and G strips to the top and bottom of the pieced center; press seams toward F and G strips.

6. Sew C to opposite sides of A to make an A-C unit as shown in Figure 7; press seams C. Repeat to make 48 A-C units.

Figure 7

7. Join 11 A-C units to make a side strip as shown in Figure 8; press seams in one direction. Repeat to make two side strips.

Figure 8

8. Repeat step 7 with 13 A-C units to make a top and bottom strip; press seams in one direction.

9. Sew C to one side and D to two adjacent sides of A to complete a corner unit as shown in Figure 9; press seams toward C and D. Repeat to make eight corner units.

Figure 9

10. Sew a corner unit to each end of each side, top and bottom strip referring to Figure 10 for positioning.

Figure 10

11. Sew a side strip to opposite sides of the pieced center, referring to the Placement Diagram for positioning of strips; press seams toward F strips. Add the top and bottom strips to the pieced center; press seams toward G strips.

12. Join three Elephant blocks with two I rectangles to make an elephant row referring to the Placement Diagram for positioning of Elephant blocks; press seams toward I rectangles. Repeat to make four elephant rows.

13. Sew an elephant row to opposite sides of the pieced center, referring to the Placement Diagram for positioning; press seams toward elephant rows.

14. Sew a J square to each end of each remaining elephant row; press seams away from the J squares.

15. Sew the elephant/J rows to the top and bottom of the pieced center to complete the pieced top; press seams toward elephant/J borders.

Completing the Quilt

1. Sandwich the batting between the completed top and prepared backing; pin or baste layers together to hold.

2. Quilt as desired by hand or machine; remove pins or basting. Trim excess backing and batting even with quilt top.

3. Join binding strips on short ends with diagonal seams to make one long strip; trim seams to ¼" and press seams open. Fold the strip in half along length with wrong sides together; press.

4. Sew binding to the right side of the quilt edges, overlapping ends. Fold binding to the back side and stitch in place. ❖

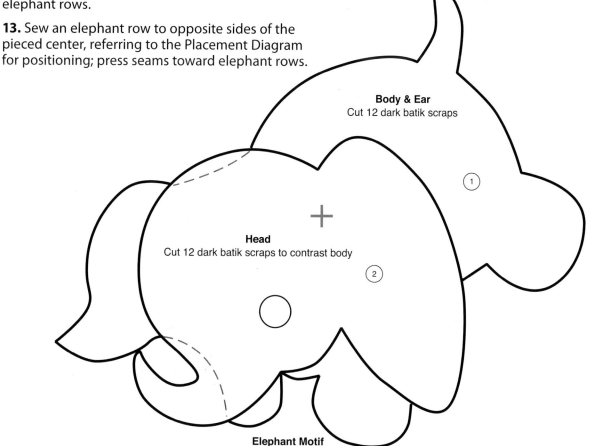

Body & Ear
Cut 12 dark batik scraps

Head
Cut 12 dark batik scraps to contrast body

Elephant Motif

Butterfly Hoedown

Combine piecing and appliqué in this happy spring-themed quilt.
Make an extra block to use in a matching tote.

Project Note

If making this quilt as a gift, the tote bag makes the perfect gift bag and will be very useful for the new mom later on.

Project Specifications

Skill Level: Advanced
Quilt Size: 50½" x 50½"
Tote Size: 13" x 12½" x 3"
Block Size: 10½" x 10½", 6" x 6"
Number of Blocks: 10 and 28

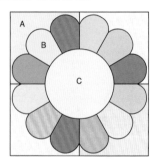

Dresden Plate
10½" x 10½" Block
Make 10

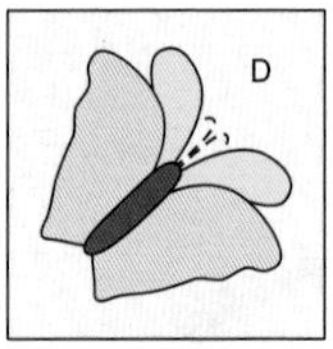

Butterfly
6" x 6" Block
Make 12

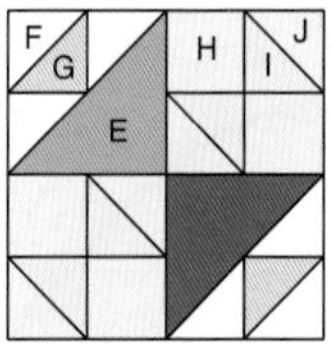

Hourglass
6" x 6" Block
Make 16

Materials (for quilt and tote)

- 6 fat quarters pastel prints for butterfly wings and B and S pieces
- Scraps brown for butterfly bodies
- Scraps medium blue prints for pieced blocks
- ⅛ yard pink print
- ¼ yard yellow dot
- ⅓ yard light green tonal
- ½ yard pink tonal
- ½ yard medium green dot
- ½ yard green/brown dot
- ⅝ yard bag lining fabric

- ⅝ yard muslin
- ¾ yard blue dot
- ⅞ yard total yellow tonals
- 1⅝ yards total light green fabrics for block backgrounds
- Quilt batting 57" x 57"
- 2 each 17" x 18" and 1¾" x 30" pieces batting
- Backing 57" x 57"
- All-purpose thread to match fabrics
- Quilting thread
- Brown embroidery floss or machine-embroidery thread
- Water-soluble marker
- Basic sewing tools and supplies

Cutting for Quilt & Tote

1. Cut (40) 5¾" x 5¾" A squares from a variety of light green fabrics.

2. Cut (12) 6½" x 6½" D squares from a variety of light green fabrics.

3. Prepare template for B and C using patterns given; cut as directed on each piece.

4. Trace butterfly shapes to make patterns for each shape. Trace shapes onto the right side of fabrics as directed on each piece for color; cut out shapes, adding a ⅛"–¼" seam allowance all around traced lines.

5. Cut three 2⅜" by fabric width strips light green tonal; subcut strips into (48) 2⅜" squares. Cut each 2⅜" square in half on one diagonal to make 96 F triangles.

6. Cut two 2⅜" by fabric width strips medium green dot; subcut strips into (32) 2⅜" squares and one 2" x 2" H square. Cut each 2⅜" square in half on one diagonal to make 64 J triangles.

7. Cut three 2" by fabric width strips medium green dot; subcut strips into (63) 2" H squares.

8. Cut one 2⅜" by fabric width strip pink print; subcut strip into (16) 2⅜" squares. Cut each square in half on one diagonal to make 32 G triangles.

9. Cut one 11" by fabric width strip pink tonal; subcut strip into (28) 1" L strips.

10. Cut two 2⅜" by fabric width strips yellow dot; subcut strips into (32) 2⅜" squares. Cut each square in half on one diagonal to make 64 I triangles.

11. Cut one 1" by fabric width strip yellow dot; subcut strip into (20) 1" K squares.

12. Cut (16) 3⅞" x 3⅞" squares medium blue scraps; cut each square in half on one diagonal to make 32 E triangles.

13. Cut two 1¾" x 34" M strips and two 1¾" x 36½" N strips blue dot.

14. Cut five 1¾" by fabric width O/P strips blue dot.

15. Cut two 3" by fabric width strips blue dot; subcut strip into two 12" Q strips and two 16" S strips.

16. Cut two 2½" by fabric width strips green/brown dot; subcut strips into two 17" R strips and one 16" S strip.

17. Cut two 4½" x 30" T strips green/brown dot.

18. Cut two 17" x 18" rectangles muslin backing.

19. Cut five assorted 2½" x 16" S strips from pastel prints.

20. Cut two 16½" x 14½" rectangles bag lining fabric.

21. Cut six 2¼" by fabric width strips yellow tonal for binding.

Butterfly Hoedown Quilt

Completing the Dresden Plate Blocks

1. Join three B pieces from bottom end to top dot as shown in Figure 1; press seams open. Repeat to make 40 B units.

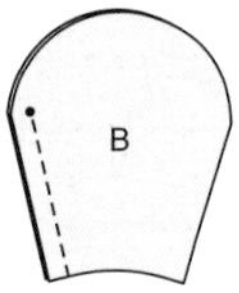

Figure 1

2. Turn under the top curved edges ¼"; baste to hold.

3. Place a B unit on an A square, matching side edges as shown in Figure 2; hand-stitch curved edges in place. Repeat to make 40 A-B units.

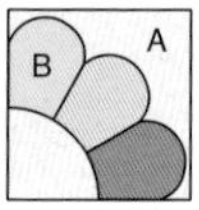

Figure 2 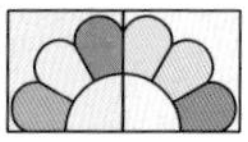   **Figure 3**

4. To complete one Dresden Plate block, select and join two A-B units to make a row as shown in Figure 3; press seams in one direction. Repeat to make two rows.

5. Join the two rows referring to Figure 4; press seam in one direction.

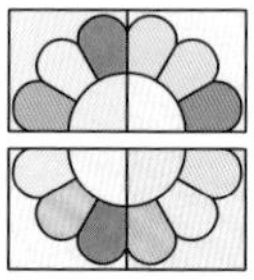

Figure 4

6. Turn under edge of C ¼" all around; baste to hold in place.

7. Center and hand- or machine-stitch C to the A-B background to complete one Dresden Plate block referring to the block drawing.

8. Repeat steps 4–7 to complete 10 Dresden Plate blocks; set one aside for tote bag.

Completing the Butterfly Blocks

1. Fold each D square on one diagonal and crease to mark the centerline.

2. Select pieces for one butterfly motif; turn under and baste edges of each piece all around (except where a piece lies under another piece).

3. Arrange and hand- or machine-stitch the basted butterfly pieces on one D square in numerical order, centering the motif on the creased line referring to the full-size pattern for positioning.

4. Repeat steps 2 and 3 to appliqué 12 butterfly motifs.

5. Mark placement of antennae on each appliquéd block using a water-soluble marker, referring to the pattern for placement.

6. Using 2 strands brown embroidery floss or brown machine-embroidery thread, straight-stitch along marked lines to complete the Butterfly blocks.

Completing the Hourglass Blocks

1. To complete one Hourglass block, sew G to F along the diagonal; press seam toward G. Repeat to make two F-G units.

2. Sew F to each G side of each F-G unit to complete two F-G corner units as shown in Figure 5; press seams toward F.

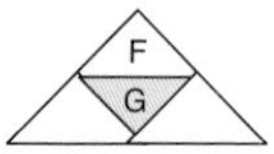

Figure 5 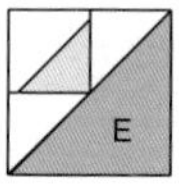   **Figure 6**

3. Sew an F-G corner unit to E to complete one E corner unit as shown in Figure 6; press seam toward E. Repeat to make two E corner units.

4. Sew I to J along the diagonal; press seam toward J; repeat to make four I-J units.

5. Sew H to the I side of each I-J unit to make four H rows as shown in Figure 7; press seams toward H.

Figure 7   **Figure 8**

6. Join two H rows to complete one H corner unit as shown in Figure 8; press seam in one direction. Repeat to make two H corner units.

7. Join one E corner unit with one H corner unit to make a row as shown in Figure 9; press seams toward E corner unit. Repeat to make two rows.

Figure 9

8. Join the rows referring to the block drawing to complete one Hourglass block; press seam in one direction.

9. Repeat steps 1–8 to complete 12 Hourglass blocks.

Completing the Top

1. Join three Dresden Plate blocks with four L strips to make a block row as shown in Figure 10; press seams toward the L strips. Repeat to make three block rows.

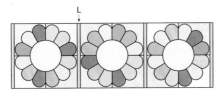

Figure 10

2. Join three L strips with four K squares to make a sashing row as shown in Figure 11; press seams toward the L strips. Repeat to make four sashing rows.

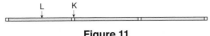

Figure 11

3. Join the block rows and the sashing rows to complete the pieced center; press seam toward the sashing rows.

4. Sew M strips to opposite sides and N strips to the top and bottom of the pieced center; press seams toward M and N strips.

5. Join two Butterfly blocks with four Hourglass blocks to make a pieced border as shown in

Figure 12; press seams in one direction. Repeat to make four pieced borders.

Figure 12

6. Sew a pieced border to opposite sides of the pieced center referring to the Placement Diagram for positioning; press seams toward M strips.

7. Sew a Butterfly block to each end of each remaining pieced border referring to Figure 13; press seams toward Butterfly blocks.

Figure 13

8. Sew a pieced border/Butterfly block to the top and bottom of the pieced center; press seams toward N strips.

9. Join the O/P strips on short ends to make one long strip; press seams open; subcut strip into two 48½" O strips and two 51" P strips.

10. Sew O to opposite sides and P to the top and bottom to complete the top; press seams toward the O and P strips.

Completing the Quilt

1. Sandwich the batting between the completed top and prepared backing; pin or baste layers together to hold.

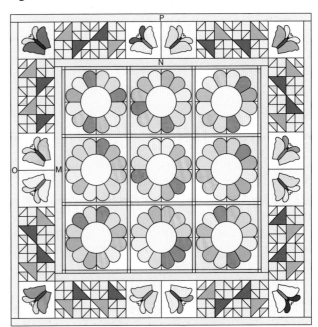

Butterfly Hoedown Quilt
Placement Diagram 50½" x 50½"

2. Quilt as desired by hand or machine; remove pins or basting. Trim excess backing and batting even with quilt top.

3. Join binding strips on short ends with diagonal seams to make one long strip; trim seams to ¼" and press seams open. Fold the strip in half along length with wrong sides together; press.

4. Sew binding to the right side of the quilt edges, overlapping ends.

5. Fold binding to the back side and hand-stitch in place to finish.

Dresden Plate Tote

1. Sew L to opposite sides of the remaining Dresden Plate block; press seams toward L strips.

2. Sew a K square to each end of two L strips; press seams toward L strips.

3. Sew a K-L strip to the top and bottom of the block; press seams toward K-L strips.

4. Sew Q to opposite sides and R to the top and bottom to complete the tote front; press seams toward Q and R strips.

5. Sandwich a 17" x 18" batting piece between the completed top and one 17" x 18" piece of muslin; pin or baste layers together to hold.

6. Quilt as desired by hand or machine.

7. Join the eight S strips along the length with the blue dot strips at each end to complete the tote back; press seams in one direction.

8. Sandwich a 17" x 18" batting piece between the completed back and one 17" x 18" piece of muslin; pin or baste layers together to hold.

9. Quilt as desired by hand or machine.

10. Trim the quilted tote front and back to 16½" x 14½".

11. Press ¼" to the wrong side on one 30" side of each T strip.

12. Place a 1¾" x 30" batting strip in the center of each pressed T strip; fold the raw edge of fabric over batting; press. Fold the pressed edge over the fabric/batting layer; press. Stitch along folded edge to secure; machine-quilt each T strip.

13. Trim ends of quilted T strips to make two 29"-long strips.

14. Pin one T strip to the right side of the top edge of the tote front leaving 6" between straps as

shown in Figure 14, machine-baste in place to hold. Repeat on the tote back.

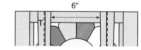

Figure 14

15. Place the 16½" x 14½" lining pieces right sides together; stitch starting at one end of one short side, across one long side and up the remaining short side, leaving a 5" opening on the last side as shown in Figure 15. Press seam to one side inserting iron inside the lining area as much as possible.

Figure 15   **Figure 16**

16. Fold the bottom corners to make a point, aligning seams as shown in Figure 16; measure and mark 1½" from point and draw a line, again referring to Figure 16. Stitch on the marked line to make square corners; trim to within ¼" from seam.

Keepsake Baby Quilts From Scraps

17. Place the tote front and back right sides together; stitch along sides and across bottom; zigzag seam edges to finish.

18. Create square corners as in step 16; zigzag edges of corner seam.

19. Place lining inside tote with right sides together and matching top edge; sew ¼" around top edge.

20. Turn the stitched unit right side out through the opening in the lining. Press lining opening edges to the inside ¼"; stitch opening closed.

21. Push lining inside tote, aligning bottom corners; press flat with iron inside tote. Press top edge.

22. Topstitch close to the top edge to finish. ❖

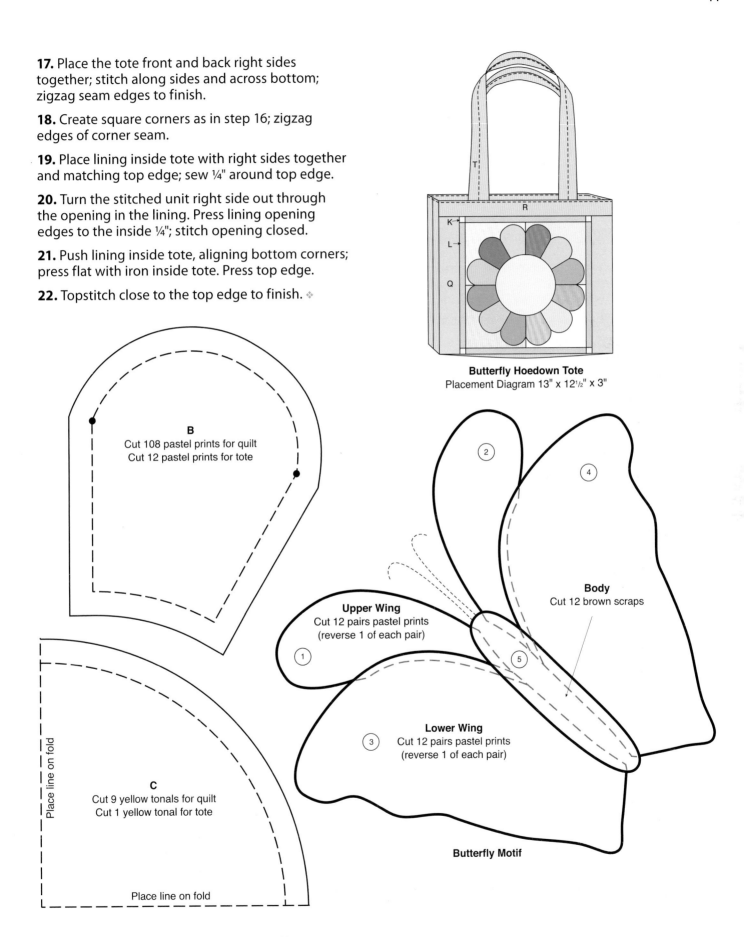

Butterfly Hoedown Tote
Placement Diagram 13" x 12½" x 3"

B
Cut 108 pastel prints for quilt
Cut 12 pastel prints for tote

C
Cut 9 yellow tonals for quilt
Cut 1 yellow tonal for tote

Place line on fold

Place line on fold

Upper Wing
Cut 12 pairs pastel prints
(reverse 1 of each pair)

Lower Wing
Cut 12 pairs pastel prints
(reverse 1 of each pair)

Body
Cut 12 brown scraps

Butterfly Motif

House of White Birches, Berne, Indiana 46711 Clotilde.com

Diamonds Royale

Whether you use templates or angled rulers, there are only three different shapes in this quick-to-stitch quilt with matching little pillows.

Project Notes

Piecing the 60-degree diamonds requires sewing with offset seams. Although not really for a beginner, simplified sewing instructions are given. To avoid separate corner and side templates, the quilt is pieced with whole diamond shapes and the excess is trimmed after piecing to square up the edges.

Diamonds Royale Quilt

Project Specifications

Skill Level: Intermediate
Quilt Size: 40½" x 50½"

Materials

- 50 (6" x 10") pastel scraps or 1 yard total
- ¼ yard gold solid
- ⅝ yard white solid
- 1⅓ yards blue paisley
- Batting 46" x 56"
- Backing 46" x 56"
- All-purpose thread to match fabrics
- Quilting thread
- 60-degree diamond template (optional)
- Basic sewing tools and supplies

Cutting

1. Prepare templates using patterns given; cut A pieces from the 6" x 10" rectangles as shown in Figure 1. *Note: If using yardage, cut seven 4½" by fabric width strips fabric; place template on strip and cut as shown in Figure 2.*

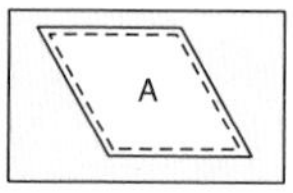

| Figure 1 | Figure 2 |

2. Cut three 1½" by fabric width strips gold solid; subcut strips into 49 B pieces referring to Figure 3.

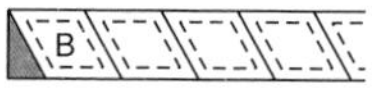

Figure 3

3. Cut five 1¼" by fabric width E strips gold solid.

4. Cut (10) 1½" by fabric width strips white solid; subcut strips into 80 C/CR pieces as shown in Figure 4. *Note: White solid has no right or wrong side, so the template does not have to be reversed to cut the CR pieces because it doesn't matter which side of the piece is used as the right side. If using a fabric with a definite right and wrong side, fold each strip in half with right sides together to make a double-layered strip. Cut using template to make a C and CR piece in one cut as shown in Figure 5.*

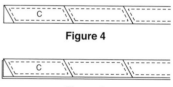

Figure 4

Figure 5

5. Cut (10) 3" by fabric width D/F strips blue paisley.

6. Cut five 2¼" by fabric width strips blue paisley for binding.

Completing the Top

1. Join nine A pieces with eight C strips to make a nine-unit row as shown in Figure 6; press seams toward C strips. Repeat to make two nine-unit rows.

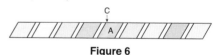

Figure 6

2. Repeat step 1 with seven A pieces and six C pieces to make a seven-unit row; press seams toward C strips. Repeat to make two seven-unit rows.

Tip

Use fabric that reads the same from either side to avoid working with mirror images for the C strips.

44

3. Join five A pieces and four C strips to make a five-unit row; press seams toward C strips. Repeat to make two five-unit rows.

4. Join three A pieces and two C strips to make a three-unit row; press seams toward C strips. Repeat to make two three-unit rows.

5. Join eight CR strips with nine B pieces to make an eight-unit sashing row as shown in Figure 7; press seams toward B.

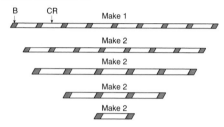

Figure 7

6. Repeat step 5 with seven CR strips and eight B pieces to make an eight-unit sashing row, again referring to Figure 7; press seams toward B. Repeat to make two seven-unit sashing rows.

7. Repeat step 5 to make two each three-unit and five unit sashing rows and two one-unit sashing rows, again referring to Figure 7.

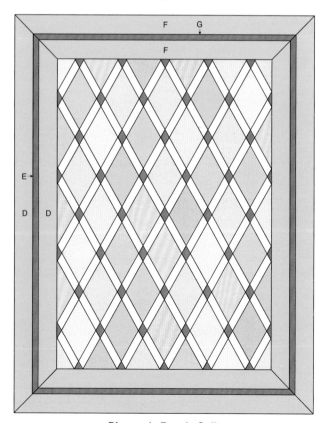

Diamonds Royale Quilt
Placement Diagram 40½" x 50½"

8. Join the sashing rows with the unit rows as shown in Figure 8 to complete the pieced center; press seams toward sashing rows.

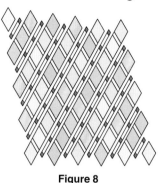

Figure 8

9. Trim excess edges, cutting ¼" below center of outside row of diamonds, as shown in Figure 9. *Note: The size should be approximately 29½" x 40½".*

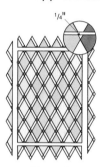

Figure 9

10. Join the D strips on short ends to make one long strip; press seams open. Subcut strip in half to make two long strips.

11. Join the E strips on short ends to make one long strip; press seams open.

12. Sew the E strip between the two D strips to make a D-E-D strip; press seams toward D strips.

13. Subcut the D-E-D strip into two 44" top/bottom strips and two 54" side strips; fold each strip in half and crease to mark the lengthwise center.

14. Fold and crease the pieced top to mark the side and top/bottom centers.

15. Center and pin the top/bottom strips to the top and bottom of the pieced center, leaving excess at each end; stitch in place, stopping stitching ¼" from edges of the pieced top as shown in Figure 10. Press seams toward strips.

Figure 10

16. Repeat step 15 with side strips on opposite long sides of the pieced center; press seams toward strips.

17. To miter corners, lay border strips flat with one on top of the other as shown in Figure 11. Twist the top strip under and away from you, creating a 45-degee angle, aligning the seams of the strips perfectly, again referring to Figure 11; press to form a creased line to use as a guide for stitching.

Figure 11

18. Fold the quilt top in half right sides together on the diagonal; starting at the unstitched seam allowance on the quilt top, stitch along the creased lines, keeping seams of strips perfectly matched as shown in Figure 12.

Figure 12

19. Trim excess to ¼" beyond seam; press seams open to complete one mitered corner as shown in Figure 13. Repeat steps 17–19 to complete all mitered corners.

Figure 13

Completing the Quilt

1. Sandwich the batting between the completed top and prepared backing; pin or baste layers together to hold.

2. Quilt as desired by hand or machine; remove pins or basting. Trim excess backing and batting even with quilt top.

3. Join binding strips on short ends with diagonal seams to make one long strip; trim seams to ¼" and press seams open. Fold the strip in half along length with wrong sides together; press.

4. Sew binding to the right side of the quilt edges, overlapping ends. Fold binding to the back side and stitch in place.

Diamonds Royale Pillow
Project Specifications
Skill Level: Intermediate
Pillow Size: 8" x 8"

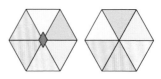

Diamonds Royale Pillow
Placement Diagram 8" x 8"

Materials
- 6 (6" x 10") pastel scraps to match quilt for each pillow
- Scrap gold solid (optional)
- All-purpose thread to match fabrics
- 60-degree diamond template (optional)
- Polyester fiberfill
- Basic sewing tools and supplies

Cutting

1. Prepare templates using patterns given; cut A pieces from the 6" x 10" rectangles as shown in Figure 1. Repeat with B pieces as desired. *Note: Sewing a B diamond piece to the center of each side of the pillow is optional.*

2. Mark the ¼" seam allowance intersection at each corner on the wrong side of each A piece as shown in Figure 14.

Figure 14

Completing the Pillow

1. Join two diamond pieces right sides together starting and stopping at the marked end points and pivoting at the marked side point as shown in Figure 15. Repeat to make three pairs.

Figure 15   **Figure 16**

2. Join the pairs, leaving a 2" opening in one seam for turning and stuffing; clip to pivot point on sides of each seam as shown in Figure 16.

3. Turn right side out through opening; poke out all points; place fiberfill in through opening until you reach the desired firmness.

Tip

Using a rotary ruler, trim the end of a fabric-width strip at an angle using the 60-degree angle line on the ruler; cut the remainder of the strip every 4½" to make the A pieces without a template as shown in Figure 17.

4. Hand-stitch the opening closed to complete one pillow.

5. If you would like to add the optional B diamond(s) over the center seams, turn and baste the edges of B to the wrong side along seam allowance.

6. Center the basted B piece(s) on the center(s) of the stitched pillow; hand-stitch in place to finish. ❖

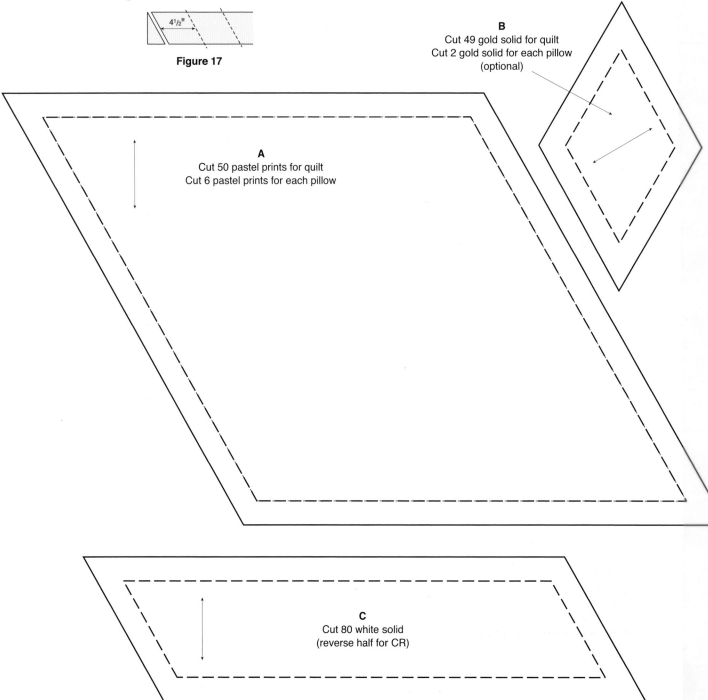

Figure 17

B
Cut 49 gold solid for quilt
Cut 2 gold solid for each pillow
(optional)

A
Cut 50 pastel prints for quilt
Cut 6 pastel prints for each pillow

C
Cut 80 white solid
(reverse half for CR)

Metric Conversion Charts

Metric Conversions

Canada/U.S. Measurement		Multiplied by	Metric Measurement
yards	x	.9144	= metres (m)
yards	x	91.44	= centimetres (cm)
inches	x	2.54	= centimetres (cm)
inches	x	25.40	= millimetres (mm)
inches	x	.0254	= metres (m)

Canada/U.S. Measurement		Multiplied by	Metric Measurement
centimetres	x	.3937	= inches
metres	x	1.0936	= yards

Standard Equivalents

Canada/U.S. Measurement	Metric Measurement	
⅛ inch	= 3.20 mm	= 0.32 cm
¼ inch	= 6.35 mm	= 0.635 cm
⅜ inch	= 9.50 mm	= 0.95 cm
½ inch	= 12.70 mm	= 1.27 cm
⅝ inch	= 15.90 mm	= 1.59 cm
¾ inch	= 19.10 mm	= 1.91 cm
⅞ inch	= 22.20 mm	= 2.22 cm
1 inch	= 25.40 mm	= 2.54 cm
⅛ yard	= 11.43 cm	= 0.11 m
¼ yard	= 22.86 cm	= 0.23 m
⅜ yard	= 34.29 cm	= 0.34 m
½ yard	= 45.72 cm	= 0.46 m
⅝ yard	= 57.15 cm	= 0.57 m
¾ yard	= 68.58 cm	= 0.69 m
⅞ yard	= 80.00 cm	= 0.80 m
1 yard	= 91.44 cm	= 0.91 m
1⅛ yards	= 102.87 cm	= 1.03 m
1¼ yards	= 114.30 cm	= 1.14 m

Canada/U.S. Measurement	Metric Measurement	
1⅜ yards	= 125.73 cm	= 1.26 m
1½ yards	= 137.16 cm	= 1.37 m
1⅝ yards	= 148.59 cm	= 1.49 m
1¾ yards	= 160.02 cm	= 1.60 m
1⅞ yards	= 171.44 cm	= 1.71 m
2 yards	= 182.88 cm	= 1.83 m
2⅛ yards	= 194.31 cm	= 1.94 m
2¼ yards	= 205.74 cm	= 2.06 m
2⅜ yards	= 217.17 cm	= 2.17 m
2½ yards	= 228.60 cm	= 2.29 m
2⅝ yards	= 240.03 cm	= 2.40 m
2¾ yards	= 251.46 cm	= 2.51 m
2⅞ yards	= 262.88 cm	= 2.63 m
3 yards	= 274.32 cm	= 2.74 m
3⅛ yards	= 285.75 cm	= 2.86 m
3¼ yards	= 297.18 cm	= 2.97 m
3⅜ yards	= 308.61 cm	= 3.09 m
3½ yards	= 320.04 cm	= 3.20 m
3⅝ yards	= 331.47 cm	= 3.31 m
3¾ yards	= 342.90 cm	= 3.43 m
3⅞ yards	= 354.32 cm	= 3.54 m
4 yards	= 365.76 cm	= 3.66 m
4⅛ yards	= 377.19 cm	= 3.77 m
4¼ yards	= 388.62 cm	= 3.89 m
4⅜ yards	= 400.05 cm	= 4.00 m
4½ yards	= 411.48 cm	= 4.11 m
4⅝ yards	= 422.91 cm	= 4.23 m
4¾ yards	= 434.34 cm	= 4.34 m
4⅞ yards	= 445.76 cm	= 4.46 m
5 yards	= 457.20 cm	= 4.57 m

E-mail: Customer_Service@whitebirches.com

Keepsake Baby Quilts From Scraps is published by DRG, 306 East Parr Road, Berne, IN 46711, telephone (260) 589-4000. Printed in USA. Copyright © 2010 DRG. All rights reserved. This publication may not be reproduced in part or in whole without written permission from the publisher.

RETAIL STORES: If you would like to carry this pattern book or any other DRG publications, call the Wholesale Department at Annie's Attic to set up a direct account: (903) 636-4303. Also, request a complete listing of publications available from DRG.

Every effort has been made to ensure that the instructions in this pattern book are complete and accurate. We cannot, however, take responsibility for human error, typographical mistakes or variations in individual work.

STAFF

Editors: Jeanne Stauffer, Sandra L. Hatch
Assistant Editor: Erika Mann
Editorial Assistant: Kortney Barile
Copy Supervisor: Michelle Beck
Copy Editors: Angie Buckles, Amanda Scheerer
Graphic Arts Supervisor: Ronda Bechinski

Graphic Artists: Pam Gregory, Erin Augsburger
Art Director: Brad Snow
Assistant Art Director: Nick Pierce
Photography Supervisor: Tammy Christian
Photography: Matthew Owen
Photo Stylist: Tammy Steiner

ISBN: 978-1-59217-287-0

1 2 3 4 5 6 7 8 9

4

8

11

14

18

22

26

32

36

40

42